BIOGRAPHIES OF DIVERSE HEROES

RUTH BADER GINSBURG

STEPHANIE GASTON

TABLE OF CONTENTS

A Crabtree Seedlings Book

School-to-Home Support for Caregivers and Teachers

This book helps children grow by letting them practice reading. Here are a few guiding questions to help the reader with building his or her comprehension skills. Possible answers appear here in red.

Before Reading:

- What do I think this book is about?
    - *I think this book is about a real person named Ruth Bader Ginsburg.*
    - *I think this book is about the important cases Ruth Bader Ginsburg sat on as the judge.*

- What do I want to learn about this topic?
    - *I want to learn more about the difficulties Ruth Bader Ginsburg faced as a Jewish woman in the legal system.*
    - *I want to learn more about her personal life.*

During Reading:

- I wonder why…
    - *I wonder why Ruth Bader Ginsburg decided that she would fight for women's rights and equality.*
    - *I wonder why Ruth Bader Ginsburg attended Harvard Law but completed her legal studies at Columbia Law.*

- What have I learned so far?
    - *I have learned that even though Ruth Bader Ginsburg was one of the best law students, she was often turned down for jobs at law firms because she was a woman.*
    - *I have learned that Ruth Bader Ginsburg was a law professor at both Rutgers University and Columbia University.*

After Reading:

- What details did I learn about this topic?
    - *I have learned that President Bill Clinton appointed Ruth Bader Ginsburg to the Supreme Court in 1993.*
    - *I have learned that she served as an Associate Justice on the Supreme Court for almost 30 years.*

- Read the book again and look for the glossary words.
    - *I see the word **advocate** on page 3 and the word **landmark** on page 14. The other glossary words are found on page 22.*

RUTH BADER GINSBURG

Ruth Bader Ginsburg was an **advocate** for women's rights and the **equality** of men and women.

Ginsburg became the first Jewish woman to serve on the Supreme Court in 1993.

Sandra Day O'Connor (seated at left) was the first woman to serve on the Supreme Court. Ruth Bader Ginsburg (standing at right) was the second woman to serve.

Ginsburg was born in New York City on March 15, 1933.

She lost both her sister and mother before finishing high school.

Ruth's mother always encouraged her to value education.

Ginsburg graduated from Cornell University at the top of her class.

She attended Harvard University but completed her legal studies at Columbia University.

She was turned down for jobs at law firms because she was a woman.

Front row, left to right: N. Boxley, G. Kalmus, L. Cohen, C. Hochman, R. Medalie, W. Kane, D. Gifford, T. Leary, P. Fishbein, R. Goodwin *(President),* J. Friedenthal, L. Starrett, A. Enker, A. Miller, C. Morse, Jr., A. Blumberg, M. Winston, J. Erens, D. Rezneck, R. Ginsburg. *Second row:* W. Kiernan, Jr., H. Schumacher, W. McGovern, Jr., P. Bennett, S. Benjamin, J. Nagin, J. Hawes, Jr., D. Page, D. Filvaroff, M. Greenberg, F. Goodman, A. Gratch, J. Winston, T. Edwards, G. Gray, III., J. Courtney, W. Milde, J. Sobeloff, G. Paschal. *Third row:* T. Ehrlich, W. Sogg, D. Dorsen, J. Anker, W. Slawson, E. Daly, Jr., A. Stein, E. Manning, H. Kenner, B. Shearer, W. Wertheimer, E. Grenier, Jr., J. R. Noall, R. Loeb, G. Greer, B. Clagett. *Missing:* R. M. Duncan, M. Eisenberg, J. Fillman, M. Grossman, R. Prosterman.

Out of 500 students attending Harvard Law School, Ginsburg was one of only nine women.

Ginsburg became a law professor at Rutgers University and later Columbia University.

She became Columbia University's first female **tenured** professor.

Ginsburg worked as a lawyer for the American Civil Liberties Union during the 1970s.

She argued six **landmark** cases on discrimination based on sex before the Supreme Court.

Ruth won five of those six cases. She argued that discrimination based on sex harms both men and women.

In 1980, Ginsburg was appointed as a judge to the U.S. Court of Appeals.

And in 1993, President Bill Clinton appointed her to the highest court in the land.

Ginsburg was an associate justice of the Supreme Court for almost 30 years.

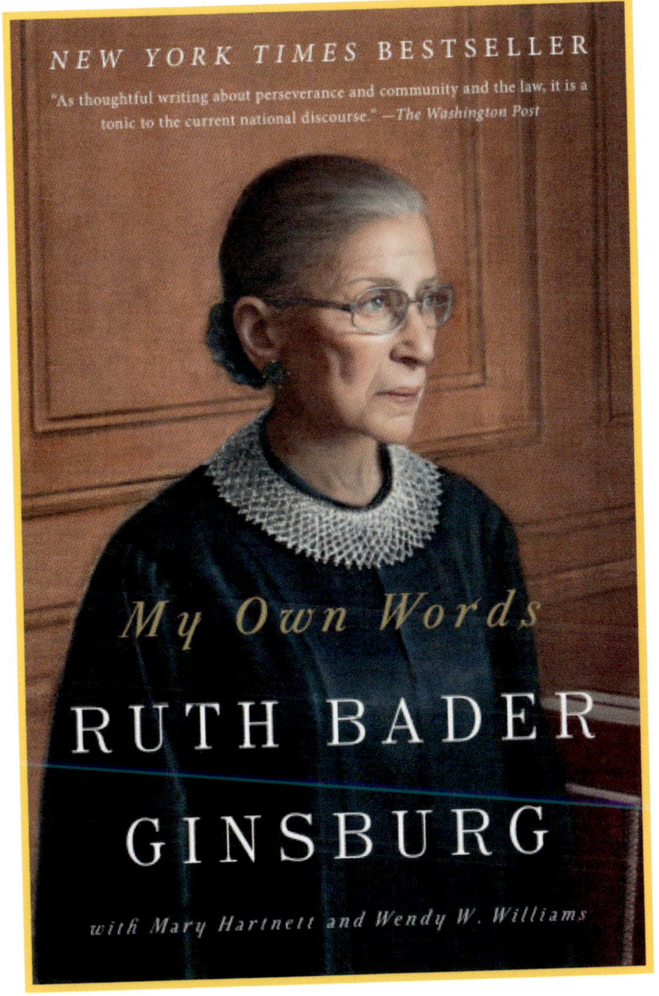

In 2016, she wrote a book about her life and career entitled *My Own Words*.

Ginsburg battled cancer for more than 20 years.

She died on September 18, 2020 at the age of 87.

USE OF REPRESENTATIVES
UNITED STATES SENATE

Glossary

advocate (ad-vuh-keyt): A person who speaks up and argues in favor of a person or cause

discrimination (dih-skrim-uh-ney-shuhn): The practice of unfairly treating a person or group of people differently from other people or groups of people

equality (ih-kwol-i-tee): The ability to enjoy the same rights and freedoms as others

landmark (land-mahrk): An important event that creates lasting change

tenured (ten-yerd): A status that gives an employee the right to keep a job for as long as they want it

Index

“Real change, enduring change, happens one step at a time.”

—Ruth Bader Ginsburg

About the Author

Stephanie Gaston is a content producer for CNN and a screenwriter. She spent more than a decade working for the FOX and ABC affiliates in Miami, Florida, before joining the ranks at CNN in 2015, ahead of an unprecedented election cycle. Stephanie is a first-generation Haitian American who grew up in Fort Lauderdale, Florida, a diverse community with Latin and Caribbean influences. Throughout her career in journalism, Stephanie has covered major stories including presidential inaugurations, natural disasters, and royal weddings. Stephanie is a dog lover, movie buff, fitness enthusiast, and most importantly, a proud mom.

Written by: Stephanie Gaston
Designed by: Under the Oaks Media
Proofreader: Petrice Custance
Print coordinator: Katherine Berti

Photographs: Steve Pettewey: cover, p. 3; dpa picture alliance: p. 5; Collection of the Supreme Court: p. 7 (top); Spiroview: p. 8; Harvard Law School Yearbook, 1958, Courtesy of Harvard Law School Library, Historical & Special Collections: p. 11; LOC: p. 13; Snipergraphics: p. 14; Lynn Gilbert: p. 15; White HOuse: p. 16 (top), 17, 21; Felix Lipov: p. 16 (bottom)

Library and Archives Canada Cataloguing in Publication

Available at the Library and Archives Canada

Library of Congress Cataloging-in-Publication Data

Available at the Library of Congress

Crabtree Publishing Company

www.crabtreebooks.com 1-800-387-7650

In Canada: We acknowledge the financial support of the Government of Canada through the Canada Book Fund for our publishing activities.

Published in the United States
Crabtree Publishing
347 Fifth Avenue
Suite 1402-145
New York, NY, 10016

Published in Canada
Crabtree Publishing
616 Welland Ave.
St. Catharines, ON
L2M 5V6

Printed in the U.S.A./072022/CG20220201